Pass **ECDL**4

Module 6: Presentation

Using Microsoft PowerPoint 2003

F.R. Heathcote

Published by

PAYNE-GALLWAY
PUBLISHERS LTD

26-28 Northgate Street, Ipswich IP1 3DB
Tel: 01473 251097 Fax: 01473 232758

www.payne-gallway.co.uk

Acknowledgements

We are grateful to WWF-UK for granting us permission to reproduce the following photograph:

Image No: 37167

Indian Tiger, Thailand © WWF-Canon / Martin Harvey

Every effort has been made to contact copyright owners of material published in this book. We would be glad to hear from unacknowledged sources at the earliest opportunity.

Cover design by Direction Advertising and Design Ltd

First Edition 2004

A catalogue entry for this book is available from the British Library.

ISBN 1 904467 34 2

Copyright © F. R. Heathcote 2004

The ECDL Trade Mark is the registered trade mark of The European Computer Driving Licence Foundation Limited in Ireland and other countries.

This ECDL Foundation approved courseware product incorporates learning reinforcement exercises. These exercises are included to help the candidate in their training for the ECDL. The exercises included in this courseware product are not ECDL certification tests and should not be construed in any way as ECDL certification tests. For information about Authorised ECDL Test Centres in different National Territories please refer to the ECDL Foundation web site at www.ecdl.com

All rights reserved

Printed in Malta by Gutenberg Press

Disclaimer

"European Computer Driving Licence" and ECDL and Stars device are registered trade marks of The European Computer Driving Licence Foundation Limited in Ireland and other countries. Payne-Gallway Publishers is an independent entity from The European Computer Driving Licence Foundation Limited, and not affiliated with The European Computer Driving Licence Foundation Limited in any manner. Pass ECDL4 Module 6 may be used in assisting students to prepare for the ECDL Module 6 examination. Neither The European Computer Driving Licence Foundation Limited nor Payne-Gallway Publishers warrants that the use of this book (Pass ECDL4 Module 6) will ensure passing the ECDL Module 6 examination. Use of the ECDL-F Approved Courseware Logo on this product signifies that it has been independently reviewed and approved by ECDL-F as complying with the following standards:

Acceptable coverage of all courseware content related to the ECDL Version 4.0.

This courseware material has not been reviewed for technical accuracy and does not guarantee that the end user will pass the ECDL Module 6 examination. Any and all assessment items and/or performance based exercises contained in this book (Pass ECDL4 Module 6) relate solely to this book and do not constitute or imply certification by The European Driving Licence Foundation in respect of any ECDL examination. For details on sitting ECDL examinations in your country please contact your country's National ECDL/ICDL designated Licensee or visit The European Computer Driving Licence Foundation Limited web site at http://www.ecdl.com.

Candidates using this courseware material should have a valid ECDL/ICDL Skills Card. Without such a Skills Card, no ECDL/ICDL Examinations can be taken and no ECDL/ICDL certificate, nor any other form of recognition, can be given to the candidate.

ECDL/ICDL Skills Cards may be obtained from any Approved ECDL/ICDL Test Centre or from your country's National ECDL/ICDL designated Licensee.

References to the European Computer Driving Licence (ECDL) include the International Computer Driving Licence (ICDL). Version 4.0 is published as the official syllabus for use within the European Computer Driving Licence (ECDL) and International Computer Driving Licence (ICDL) certification programme.

Preface

Who is this book for?

This book is suitable for anyone studying for ECDL Version 4.0 (Module 6), either at school, adult class or at home. It is suitable for complete beginners or those with some prior experience, and takes the learner step-by-step from the very basics to the point where they will feel confident using Microsoft PowerPoint to create many different kinds of presentation to be delivered using a computer, an overhead projector or in the form of handouts.

The approach

The approach is very much one of "learning by doing". Each module is divided into a number of chapters which correspond to one lesson. The student is guided step-by-step through a practical task at the computer, with numerous screenshots to show exactly what should be on their screen at each stage. Each individual in a class can proceed at their own pace, with little or no help from a teacher. At the end of most chapters there are exercises which provide invaluable practice. By the time a student has completed the module, every aspect of the ECDL syllabus will have been covered.

Software used

The instructions and screenshots are based on a PC running Microsoft Windows XP and Microsoft PowerPoint 2003. However, it will be relatively easy to adapt the instructions for use with other versions of PowerPoint.

Extra resources

Answers to practice exercises and other useful supporting material can be found on the publisher's web site www.payne-gallway.co.uk/ecdl.

About ECDL

The European Computer Driving Licence (ECDL) is the European-wide qualification enabling people to demonstrate their competence in computer skills. Candidates must study and pass the test for each of the seven modules listed below before they are awarded an ECDL certificate. The ECDL tests must be undertaken at an accredited test centre. For more details of ECDL tests and test centres, visit the ECDL web site www.ecdl.com.

Module 1: Concepts of Information Technology

Module 2: Using the Computer and Managing Files

Module 3: Word Processing

Module 4: Spreadsheets

Module 5: Database

Module 6: Presentation

Module 7: Information and Communication

Module 6
Presentation

In this module you will find out how to use presentation tools on a computer. You will learn how to:

- create a presentation using different slide layouts for display and printed distribution
- format and modify presentations
- insert images, charts and drawn objects into a presentation
- duplicate and move text, pictures, images and charts within a presentation
- duplicate and move text, pictures, images and charts between presentations
- use various slide show effects

Module 6   Table of Contents

The Basics

What is Microsoft PowerPoint?

Microsoft PowerPoint is the leading graphics presentation package. You can use it to create, design and organise professional presentations quickly and easily.

Planning a presentation

To deliver an effective presentation you need to consider who your audience is, and prepare your slides to suit them.

Whoever your presentation is for, here are a few basic guidelines:

❶ Start with a title screen showing what the project is about.

❶ Don't put more than 4 or 5 bullets on each slide. People can't concentrate on too much information at once.

❶ Keep each point short and simple. You may want to talk around each point to explain it in further detail.

❶ Sound, graphics and animation can add interest, but don't overdo them!

Getting started

◉ Load **Microsoft PowerPoint**. You can do this in one of two ways:

◉ *Either* double-click the **PowerPoint** icon

◉ *Or* click **Start** at the bottom left of the screen, then click **All Programs**, then click

🖳 Microsoft PowerPoint

Your screen will look like the one below:

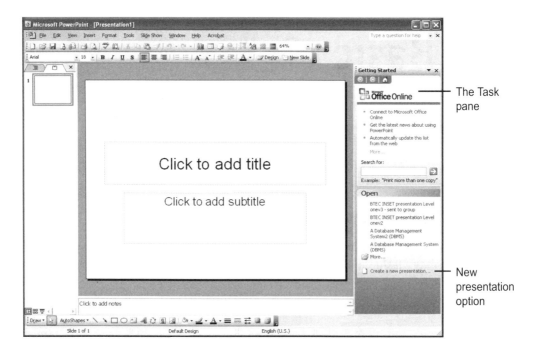

The Task pane

New presentation option

The Task pane

On the right of the screen is the Task pane. If you can't see this pane:

○ Go to **View**, **Task pane** on the Main Menu bar at the top of the screen.

This pane should appear every time you open PowerPoint, and it contains a list of commonly used commands. At each stage of your presentation, PowerPoint will display different menus in this Task pane. You should find this very useful, as the contents of the menu changes according to what you are doing, so it displays the most relevant options.

❶ If you want to see the different menus that can appear in the Task pane, or switch to a particular menu, just click the small down-arrow at the top of the Task pane, then click to select the menu that you want.

Click here to view the different Task panes

Tip:
You have probably come across the Task pane in other Office 2003 or XP applications.

Starting a blank presentation

○ Click **Create a new presentation** in the Task pane.

○ Click **Blank Presentation** in the **New Presentation** pane.

You will notice that the Task pane automatically changes to display the **Slide Layout** options.

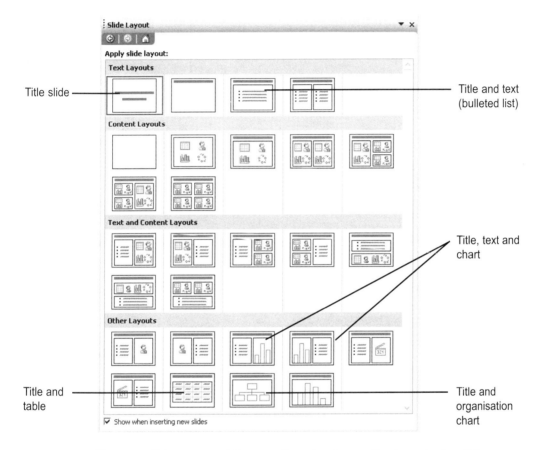

Title slide

Title and text (bulleted list)

Title, text and chart

Title and table

Title and organisation chart

You can click on one of these options to change the layout of a slide.

PowerPoint has automatically selected the **Title Slide** layout, which is exactly what we want. The boxes marked out on the screen are called **Placeholders**. These show where you will place your text and graphics.

Toolbars

You will learn about what individual toolbars and buttons do as they become relevant whilst you are creating your presentation. The tips that follow apply to all toolbars, and will be useful if you cannot find a particular toolbar or think that you are missing a button or two! You may find that you already know most of this – it will be pretty much the same as you have experienced in other Microsoft applications such as **Word** or **Excel**.

Hiding and displaying toolbars

You can select which toolbars are displayed on your screen. If you find that you can't find a particular button it might be worth checking that you have the right toolbars displayed.

○ Select **View**, **Toolbars** and select the toolbar you want from the list that appears.

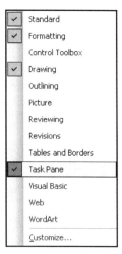

Modifying basic options

There are a number of options that users can select in PowerPoint. These are found in the **Options** dialogue box – let's have a look.

○ Select **Tools**, **Options** from the main menu.

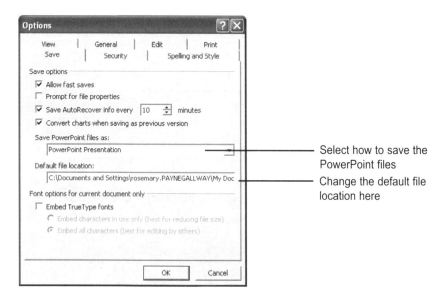

Select how to save the PowerPoint files

Change the default file location here

○ Click the **Save** tab and you can select how to save PowerPoint files (i.e. as a web page or as a particular version of PowerPoint presentation) and the default location for saving your files e.g. My Documents folder.

○ Click the **General** tab and you can change the user name (i.e. the author name listed under the file properties).

Using the Help functions

If at any time you aren't sure how to do something in **PowerPoint**, you can search the Help files for instructions on your chosen subject. For example, let's search for help on **copying** and **pasting**.

○ Select **Help, Microsoft Office PowerPoint Help** from the menu.

You will see the PowerPoint Help window appear.

○ Type **copying and pasting** into the **Search for:** box, then click the **Start Searching** button.

○ Select **Copy and paste text** from the next pop-up box.

A **Help** window appears giving information on this topic.

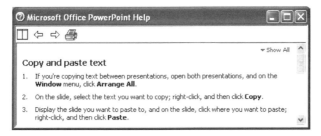

○ Click the red **Close** icon to close the **Help** window.

○ Click the black **Close** icon to close the Task pane.

Click here to close the Task pane

Adding text to the title slide

○ Click in the box marked **Click to add title** and type the title **Conserving Tigers in the Wild**.

○ Now add a sub-title. Click where indicated and type **Framework and Strategy for Action 2003**.

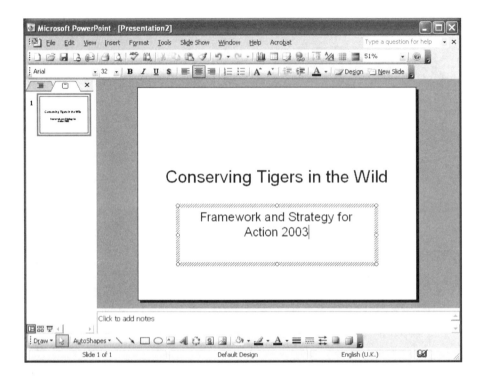

Tip:
To see what each button on the toolbar is called, just place the cursor over that button for a few seconds and the name should pop up.

Formatting and moving the text

You can click the text boxes to move them around the screen. You can also format the text in each text box just like you would in **Microsoft Word** – for example, change its colour, size or alignment.

Most of the commands you will need for this will be on the Formatting toolbar. Some of the most frequently used buttons are labelled below:

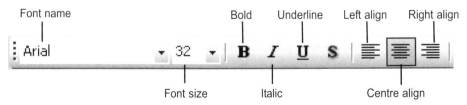

To format text you need to select the text box by clicking its border. When the border has changed from a diagonal striped box to a fuzzy one you know you can start formatting the text.

If you want to edit, add or delete text in a box, click inside the box. The border changes to diagonal stripes.

Diagonally striped border — Frame   Frame — Fuzzy border

○ Select the sub-title text box so that it has a fuzzy border.

○ Change the font to **Times New Roman** by clicking the down-arrow in the **Font** box on the Formatting toolbar and choosing it from the list that appears.

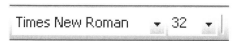

Times New Roman ▾ 32 ▾

I ——○ Make the text italic by clicking on the **Italic** button.

Tip:
To change the case of selected text, select **Format, Change Case**.

The text is already centred left and right, but not top and bottom. We will do this now:

○ Make sure the text box is selected then right-click anywhere on the text.

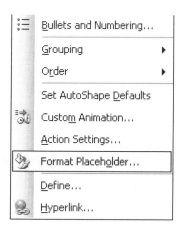

Bullets and Numbering...
Grouping ▸
Order ▸
Set AutoShape Defaults
Custom Animation...
Action Settings...
Format Placeholder...
Define...
Hyperlink...

○ Click to select the option **Format Placeholder** (this text box is actually called a **Placeholder** because it is part of the **Slide Layout**, but it is essentially the same as a text box).

○ Select the **Text Box** tab, then select **Middle** from the dropdown list for **Text Anchor Point**.

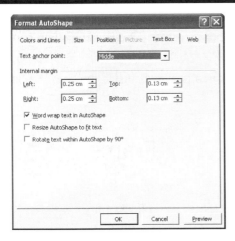

● Click **OK** to close the dialogue box.

The text should now be centred both ways in the text box (or placeholder).

Resizing and moving text boxes and placeholders

It would be nice if the sub-title text appeared on one line rather than two, but without making the text smaller. To do this we will alter the size of the text box using the **handles**.

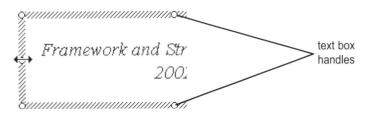

text box handles

● Move the cursor over the left-hand handle so that it becomes an arrow like in the screenshot above.

● Click and drag the handle to make the text box wider. Repeat this until the text fits on one line. Don't worry that it is now a bit too far left.

● Now move the text box back to the centre by moving the cursor over the text box border somewhere where there is no handle, so the cursor becomes a cross:

● Click and drag the box until it looks central. Click outside the text box to deselect it.

Tip:
To delete a text box, click its border to select it and then press the **Delete** key. To delete part of the contents of a text box, highlight the text to be removed and then press the **Delete** key.

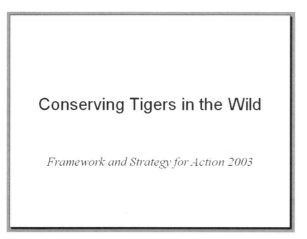

Changing the presentation view

You can alternate between various views of the presentation by clicking on the icons at the bottom of the screen (left-hand side).

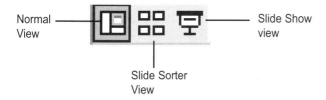

Normal View — | | — Slide Show view

Slide Sorter View

Normal View

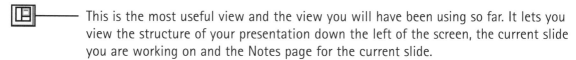

This is the most useful view and the view you will have been using so far. It lets you view the structure of your presentation down the left of the screen, the current slide you are working on and the Notes page for the current slide.

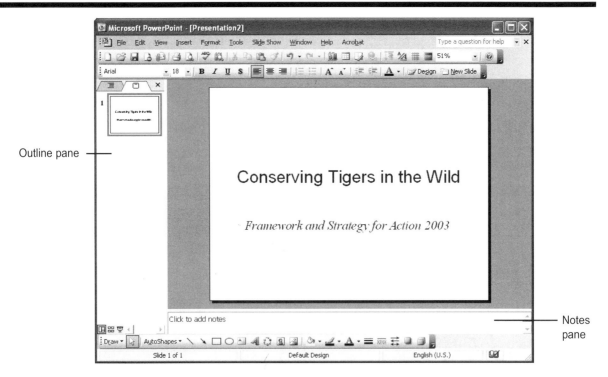

❶ The Outline pane has two different views – one view shows a picture of all the slides, and the other just lists the text on each slide. Click on the tabs at the top of the Outline pane to switch between the views.

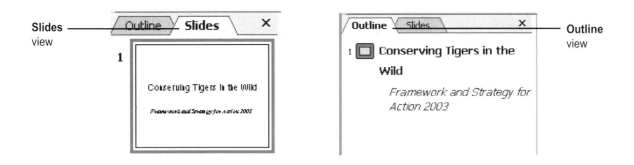

Slide Sorter View

 This view helps you to organise your slides in later stages. You will use this view later when you have more than one slide. Here's a preview of what it will look like when you have more slides:

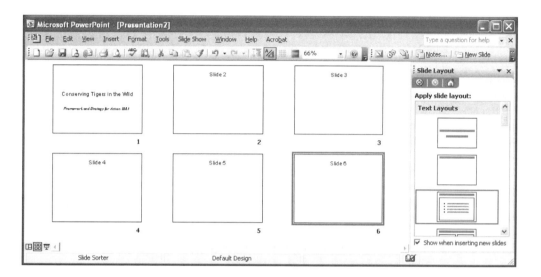

Slide Show

This is the view you use when you are actually giving your presentation.

 ● Click this icon to view your presentation so far.

● Exit the presentation by pressing the **Esc** key.

Using the Zoom tool

You can change the size of the slide in **Normal View** by using the **Zoom** tool on the **Standard** toolbar.

Zoom

● To make the slide appear much bigger, either type **200** into the **Zoom** box or select **200%** from the list that appears when you click the small down-arrow.

● This is much bigger than we want it for now! Most of the time you will probably just want the slide to fit into the window. To do this, click the small down-arrow on the **Zoom** tool, and select **Fit** from the list.

The Undo, Redo and Repeat commands

Undo

 At any time, if you do something that you didn't mean to, or don't like, just click the **Undo** button. This will undo your most recent action; you can click it more than once to undo more than one action.

Redo

 If you undo something you didn't mean to, just click the **Redo** button! If you haven't recently used the **Undo** button, the **Redo** button won't be active.

Repeat

If you want to repeat an action, for example adding a bullet point or inserting a slide, you can use the **Repeat** command. To do this select **Edit**, **Repeat** from the menu. If the action is not repeatable, the repeat command won't appear in the menu.

Saving your presentation

> ●   Click **File** on the menu bar and select **Save**.

We'll create a new folder to save your presentation in.

> ●   Use the arrow next to the **Save in** box to navigate to the location for your new folder.

> ●   Create a new folder to save your presentation by clicking the **Create New Folder** button.

> ●   Enter **Tiger Presentation** as the folder name.

> ●   Enter **Tigers** as the **File name**.

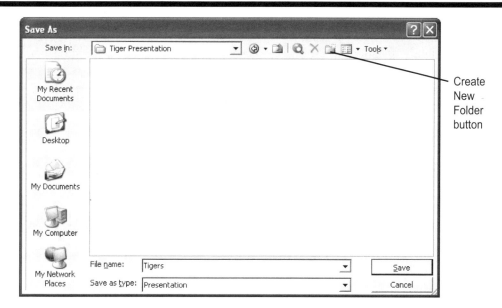

Create
New
Folder
button

○ PowerPoint will automatically save the file as a **Presentation (*.ppt)** file type. This
  is what we want for now.

 ───○ Click the **Save** button.

Closing the file and application

○ To close your presentation select **File**, **Close** from the menu.

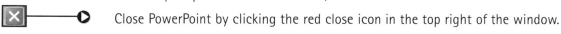 ───○ Close PowerPoint by clicking the red close icon in the top right of the window.

Tip:

You can close files and applications by clicking the red cross at the top right of
each window. When closing your presentation, be careful not to confuse the
presentation **Close** icon with the PowerPoint application **Close** icon.

Exercise

You are employed in the Human Resources department of a (fictitious) company which produces and sells maps of different European countries. You are asked to create a PowerPoint presentation that can be used for the induction of new staff. This should provide information about the company and its markets. You will develop this presentation in later end of chapter exercises.

1.   Load PowerPoint and enter a main heading **Mapsters UK Ltd** on a title slide. Make this heading Arial, bold size 54.

2.   Enter a sub-title **Information for new company employees**. Change the font to Forte, bold, size 32.

3.   Adjust the size of the text box for the sub-title so that it fits on one line.

4.   Centre the sub-title vertically in the text box.

5.   Create a new folder called **Presentations**.

6.   Save the company presentation as **Mapsters.ppt** in your new folder.

Mapsters UK Ltd

Information for new company employees

Editing a Show

In this chapter you'll add some more content to, and edit, the presentation you started in Chapter 6.1.

Opening an existing presentation

▶ Load **PowerPoint**.

You may see the **Tigers.ppt** presentation listed in the Task pane. Clicking this would open your presentation but for practice we will open it a different way.

▶ Click on the option **File**, **Open** from the main menu.

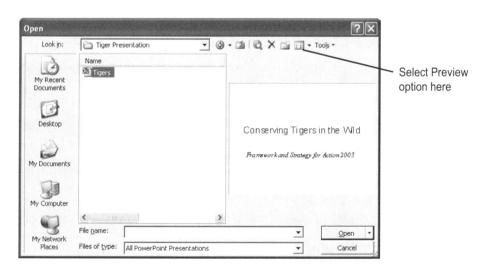

Select Preview option here

▶ Find the presentation by first locating the **Tiger Presentation** folder in the **Look in:** dropdown list.

▶ When you have found it, click to select it then click **Open**.

▶ Make sure you are in **Normal View** by clicking the **Normal View** button at the bottom of the screen.

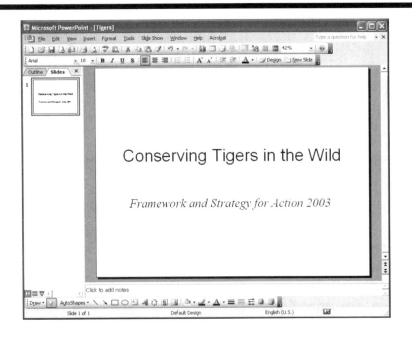

Starting a new slide

Now you can begin the second slide of the presentation.

New Slide ► Click the **New Slide** button on the **Standard** toolbar.

The **Slide Layout** has already been selected by PowerPoint – it has guessed that we want the **Title and Text** layout and it's right!

► Enter the text as shown on the following screenshot, remembering to press **Enter** each time you start a new point.

Contents

- The Challenge – Key Threats
- Current Population Estimates
- The Response – Planned Action
- Funding

Changing text size

You can increase or decrease the size of text by using the **Font Size** buttons on the Formatting toolbar.

○ Select all of the bulleted text on the current slide.

 ○ Click several times on the **Increase Font Size** button to increase the size of the text.

Tip:

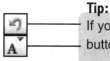 If you make the text too big, you can make it smaller either by clicking the **Undo** button or the **Decrease Font Size** button.

Changing line spacing

The text could do with being more spread out. You can increase or decrease the line spacing using the **Increase** and **Decrease Paragraph Spacing** buttons.

 ○ With the bulleted text highlighted, click the **Increase Paragraph Spacing** button until the text fills the text box.

Your screen should now look something like the one below:

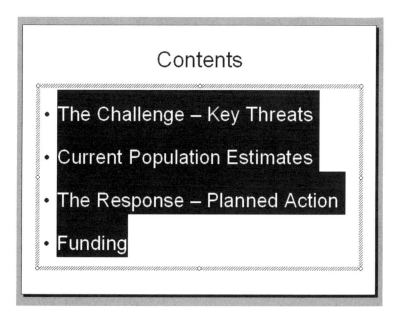

Checking your spelling

 ○ Check your spelling either by using the main menu (**Tools, Spelling**) or by clicking the **Spelling** button on the **Standard** toolbar.

PowerPoint will try to correct all the words it has underlined in red. These may be words that it thinks are spelt incorrectly or repeated words.

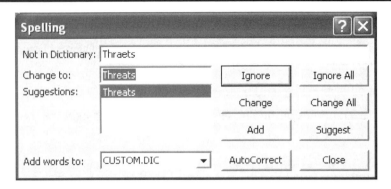

- ○ Click on the correct spelling in the **Suggestions** box and then click **Change**. (If the correct spelling does not appear you will have to type it into the **Change to** box.)

- ○ If the spell-check picks up a repeated word, click **Change** to delete it.

- ○ If the spell-check picks up a word that is actually correct (e.g. a name) then click **Ignore**.

- ○ When the spell-check is complete, click **OK**.

Adding more slides

You are going to add more slides to your presentation, this time using the **Outline** pane.

- ○ In the **Outline** pane, make sure the **Slides** tab is selected then click on the first slide.

 ○ Click the **New Slide** button to add a slide. PowerPoint automatically adds this slide after the first slide because the first slide was selected.

- ○ Click the **New Slide** button **two** more times. Don't worry about the **Slide Layout** just now – we will edit that later.

Adding titles

- ○ In the **Outline** pane, click the **Outline** tab then click the **Slide 2** icon so that slide 2 appears in the main window.

- ○ Enter the text **The Challenge – Key Threats** either on the slide where it says to add the title, or if you just start typing while the **Slide 2** icon is selected you can type it straight into the **Outline** pane.

- ○ Enter the other titles in the same way so that your Outline pane looks like the one on the next page.

- ❶ Try pressing the **Return** key after entering a title; PowerPoint will automatically insert a new slide. You can then easily delete the slide by clicking it in the **Outline** pane and pressing the **Delete** key.

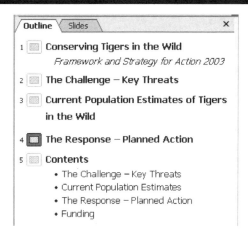

Changing the order of slides

You may have noticed that since adding those extra slides, the contents slide is now at the end of the presentation – we want it to be immediately after **Slide 1**.

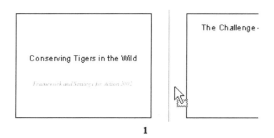

- It is easiest to move slides around in **Slide Sorter View,** so click the **Slide Sorter View** icon.

- Click on **Slide 5** and hold down the mouse button. Drag the **Contents** slide (**Slide 5**) so that a grey vertical line appears after **Slide 1** as shown below. Drop the slide here.

Your slides should now be in the right order!

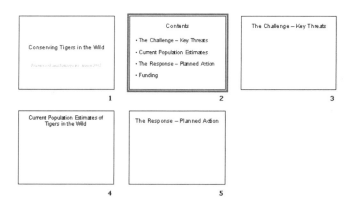

Now we'll add some more text to **Slide 3**.

- From **Slide Sorter View**, double-click **Slide 3**. This should display **Slide 3** in **Normal View**.

- Enter the text for the first bullet point as **Poaching Driven by Illegal Wildlife Trade**. Click **Enter**.

We want this next bullet to be indented a little. To move bullets to the right or left of the screen you use the **Promote** and **Demote** buttons on the **Outlining** toolbar.

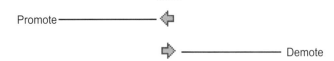

Promote ——————————— ⬦

⬦ ——————————— Demote

- To display the Outlining toolbar, select **View**, **Toolbars** and click on **Outlining**. It is normally displayed down the left of the Outline pane.

- Move the bullet to the right by clicking the **Demote** button.

- Enter the text **Ban on International Trade of Tiger Parts**. Click **Enter**. You will notice that the text will be a bit smaller than on the first bullet point.

The next bullet point will automatically follow the format of the previous one, which is what we want.

- Enter the text **Human Pressure on Habitats** as the second sub-point.

- Enter the rest of the text on the slide so that it looks like the slide below. You will have to click the **Promote** button to restore the bullets to the left of the slide.

The Challenge – Key Threats

- Poaching Driven by Illegal Wildlife Trade
  - Ban on International Trade of Tiger Parts
  - Human Pressure on Habitats
- Habitat Loss and Fragmentation
- Inadequate International Cooperation
- Funding Constraints

Customising bullets

You can change the style and colour of bullets to increase the impact of subset points.

◉ Highlight the text of the two demoted bullets. Select **Format, Bullets and Numbering** from the main menu.

A selection of commonly used bullets is shown in the **Bullets and Numbering** window.

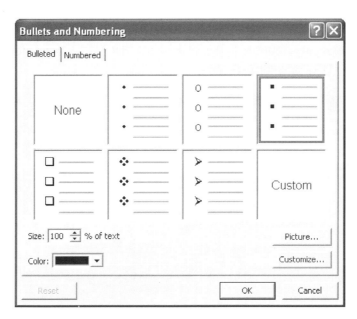

◉ Click to select a new shape for your bullets. Click **OK** to close the dialogue box.

Tip:
To change a bulleted list to a numbered list, highlight the bullet points and click the **Numbering** button on the Formatting toolbar. To change the style of numbering (e.g. i, ii, iii or 1), 2), 3)), select **Format, Bullets and Numbering** from the main menu. Click the **Numbered** tab, select a numbering style and then click **OK**.

Moving text lines around

The bullet point **Human Pressure on Habitats** should actually be under the bullet point **Habitat Loss and Fragmentation**. Move it down to its new place as follows:

Tip:
You will need to do this in Outline view in the Outline pane. To change to Outline view from Slides view, just click the **Outline** tab at the top of the Outline pane.

◉ Click the mouse pointer to the left of **Human Pressure on Habitats** in the **Outline** pane and you will see a four-headed arrow style pointer.

◐ Hold the mouse button down and drag downwards. A line will appear across the text. Keep dragging until the line is underneath **Habitat Loss and Fragmentation** and then release the mouse button.

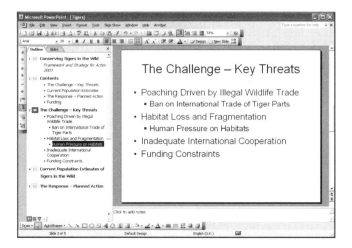

The text should have moved down the slide.

❶ You can move text from one slide to another in exactly the same way! Have a go at moving text from one slide to another. Just click the **Undo** button when you are done to restore the slide as shown above.

Checking your presentation

You can view your progress so far. Look at it first in **Slide Sorter** view.

◐ Click the **Slide Sorter View** button at the bottom of the screen.

When you click the **Slide Show** button the presentation starts at the selected slide (the one with the black border).

◐ Click the first slide to select it and then click the **Slide Show** button.

◐ Click or press the **Space bar** to move to the next slide.

Pressing the **Backspace** key goes back one slide. Remember you can exit your presentation at any time by pressing the **Esc** key.

Take a break!

◐ Save your presentation using the **Save** icon and then close the presentation.

Exercise

At the end of Chapter 6.1 you began producing a presentation for the induction of new employees at Mapsters UK Ltd. You will now add more slides to the presentation, edit slides and practise running the slide show.

1. Open the file **Mapsters.ppt**.

2. Start a new slide that has a simple title and text layout. Insert a heading **Company History**.

3. Change the size of the text in the bullet points to 22 and enter the following:

   Company (formally known as European Maps UK Ltd) founded in 1920 by George G Girling

   Early work concentrated on industrial and topographic wall maps for the educational market

   In 1961 production moved to tourist maps

   Mapsters series for tourists now comprises 10 maps

   Latest developments – Graphical Information Systems (GIS)

4. Increase the line spacing between the bullet points so that the text box is filled. Run the spell-checker and make any necessary corrections.

5. Add the following titles to four new slides.

   Company Organisation

   Sales by Product

   Target Markets

   Contents

6. Add the following bullet points to the last slide:

   - **Company History**
   - **Company Organisation**
   - **Sales by Product**
   - **Target Markets**

7. Move the last slide (**Contents**) to become the second slide.

8. Change the order of slides 5 and 6.

9. Change the order of the text on slide 2 – swap lines 3 and 4.

10. Run the slide show, then save and close your presentation.

Applying Designs

Now we'll look at the overall appearance of the slides. The slides could do with brightening up a bit to increase the impact of the presentation. We'll also insert some pictures to add interest.

◉   Open the **Tigers** presentation.

Designing the Master Slide

The **Master Slide** is a slide that dictates the format of every other slide in your presentation. For example, if you choose a particular background colour and font for the **Master Slide**, this background colour and font will appear on all your slides. It's rather like a template in **Word**, or even the header and footer in **Word** – whatever you type in as the header and footer in **Word** appears on every page – and the same is true in **PowerPoint** with the **Master Slide**.

◉   View the **Master Slide** by selecting **View**, **Master**, **Slide Master** from the menu.

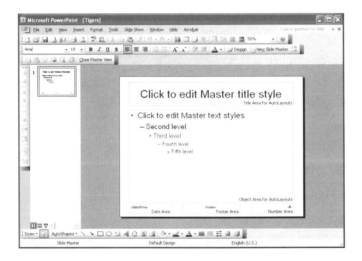

We will first put a coloured background on the slide. There are two ways to add a background design – you can either select a colour and a fill effect, or you can choose from a range of pre-designed backgrounds, or **Design Templates**.

Design Templates

Design —● Click the **Slide Design** button on the **Formatting** toolbar.

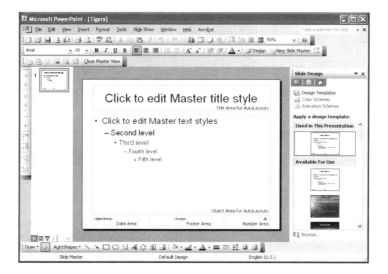

The **Slide Design** pane appears. There are options for **Design Templates**, **Colour Schemes** and **Animation Schemes**.

● Make sure the **Design Templates** option is selected. You will see a large variety of design templates available.

● Choose a design that you like, then click to select it.

● It's very easy to try a different template if you change your mind – just click a different one!

● Now view your presentation in **Slide Sorter** view by clicking the **Slide Sorter View** button.

It should look a bit more colourful now!

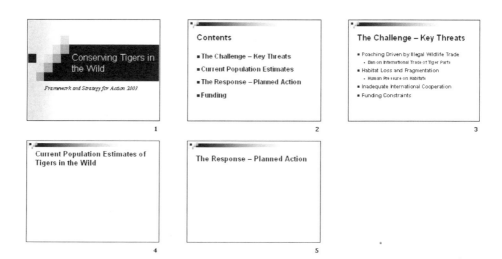

Changing the slide background colour

You can change the background colour of a slide. If the slide already has a design template selected for it, then you can change the colour of the template; if there is no template then you can just change the colour of the plain background. In fact, if you look in the list of design templates you will see that even the plain white background is a design template – just a very simple one! So to make a plain colour background, you can choose the plain design template then change the colour of the plain template.

> ● Make sure the **Slide Design** pane is visible. Change to **Normal View** with **Slide 2** selected.

> ● Suppose we want to lighten the colour of the template, but keep the same pattern. Click where it says **Color Schemes** at the top of the **Slide Design** pane.

> ● We'll chose a dark blue background colour only for the selected slide. To apply it just to the selected slide, click the small down-arrow that appears on each scheme when you move mouse over it.

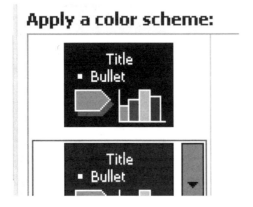

> ● Click to select the option **Apply to Selected Slides**. The current slide should change colour. If you don't like the new colour just click **Undo**.

❶ If you wanted to change the scheme for all slides, you would select the **Apply to All Slides** option.

❶ If you wanted this to be just a plain dark blue background without the pattern, you would have to change the **Design Template** to a plain one **before** choosing the colour scheme.

Plain design template —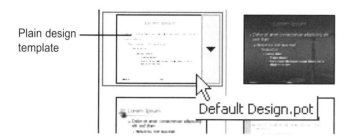

Adding page numbers

You can add page numbers to just one slide, some slides or all slides. You can also choose to have them only on the Notes pages and not on the actual slides. You can add page numbers whilst you are in **Normal View** or in the **Slide Master**.

◉ Select **View**, **Header and Footer** from the menu.

The **Header and Footer** dialogue box has options for adding a **Date/Time** field and **Footer** text as well as page numbers.

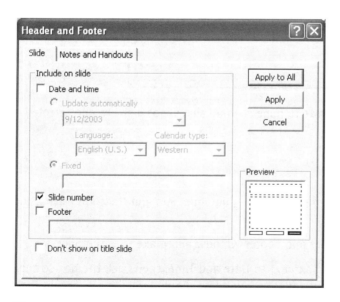

◉ Make sure your settings look like those in the screenshot above – with only the **Slide number** box checked.

◉ You have the option to apply these settings only to the slide that is selected, or to all of them. We want page numbers on every page, so click **Apply to All**.

Adding text to the header and footer

You can add text to the header and footer in just the same way as in **Word** and **Excel**. You can choose whether the footer text appears on just the selected slide, or on all slides in your presentation. We will add the text **World Tiger Conservation Fund 2003** to the footer.

○ To add a footer, you use the same window as for the page numbers, so open the **Header and Footer** window by selecting **View, Header and Footer**.

○ We want the footer to appear on the slides, rather than the notes and handouts, so make sure the **Slide** tab is selected at the top of the window.

○ Click in the **Footer** checkbox to activate the footer. You can now add the text **World Tiger Conservation Fund 2003** in the box provided.

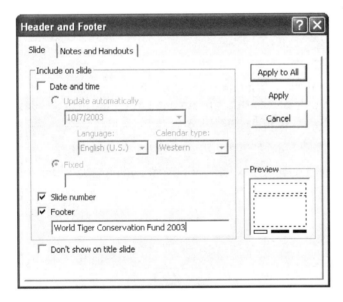

○ You want the text to appear on all slides, not just the one selected, so click **Apply to All**.

Adding a date to slides

This is done in the same way as the page numbers and the footer using the **Header and Footer** window.

○ Open the **Header and Footer** window and make sure the **Slide** tab is selected.

○ Click the checkbox next to **Date and Time**, then click the box so that the date updates automatically. Your window should look like the one in the next screenshot.

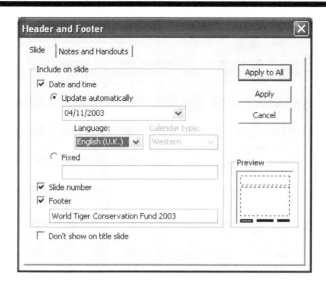

○ Click the **Apply to All** button.

○ View all these changes by clicking the **Slide Show** button.

Tip:
If you don't want the date to be updated automatically, uncheck the **Update automatically** option in the dialogue box shown above.

Repositioning the footer, date and page numbers

Notice that the footer goes onto two lines – it would look neater on one. To reposition this you use the **Slide Master**.

○ View the **Slide Master** by clicking **View, Master, Slide Master**.

More than one master slide?

The Design Template automatically creates two Slide Masters, one for the Title slide and one for all the others.

○ Click to select the master slide in the **Outline** pane that represents the non-title slides.

○ Notice that there are marked-out areas for the **Date Area**, **Footer Area** and **Number Area**. To move the boundaries of each area, click in the area, then use the handles to drag the outline to where you want it.

◉   Adjust the areas so that your screen looks like the one below:

◉   Return to **Normal View** by selecting **View, Normal** from the menu.

Changing the layout of a slide

At any point you can change the layout of a slide, even if you have already entered text. The fourth slide **Current Population Estimates of Tigers in the Wild** will contain a graph, not bullet points, so the layout needs to be changed.

◉   Go to **Slide 4** by clicking on it in the **Outline** pane.

◉   View the **Slide Layout** pane by selecting **Format, Slide Layout** from the menu.

◉   Click to select the **Title and Chart** layout from the list.

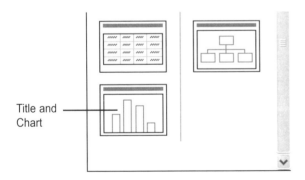

Title and Chart

The text **Double click to add chart** will appear in the middle of the bottom placeholder, but we won't create the graph just yet.

Layouts that include Clip Art

The fifth slide will have a picture as well as text, so first you must change its layout.

◗ In the **Outline** pane select **Slide 5**.

◗ Make sure the **Slide Layout** pane is visible then select the layout named **Title, Text and Clip Art**.

Tip:
If you hold the cursor over a layout, the tool tip will appear with the name of that layout.

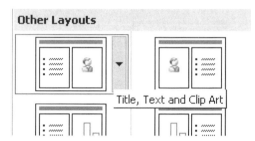

Your slide should now look like the one below:

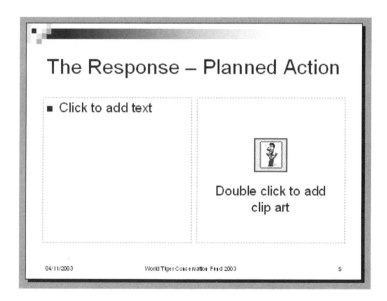

We will insert some Clip Art in the next chapter.

Tip:
If you wanted to insert an image from another file into a normal slide, you wouldn't need to change the layout. Simply select **Insert, Picture, From file**. Locate the image file and click **Insert**. To delete the image, click to select it and press the **Delete** key.

Creating an organisation chart

Drawing an **organisation chart** is very straightforward if you use the layout provided by **PowerPoint**. We will create a chart showing the structure of the World Tiger Conservation Fund.

 ◗   Create a new slide by clicking the **New Slide** button.

◗   View the slide in **Normal View**.

◗   If the **Slide Layout** pane is not visible, select **Format**, **Slide Layout** from the menu.

 ◗   Scroll down until you see the **Title and Diagram or Organization Chart** layout, then click to select it.

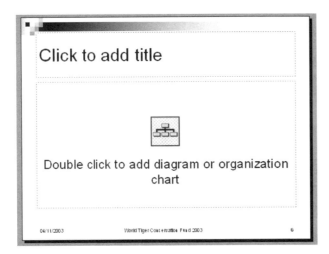

◗   Add the slide title **The Organisation Structure** and centre the text.

◗   Double-click where it says to create an organisation chart.

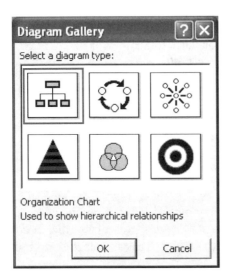

◗   Make sure the first option, **Organization Chart** is selected. Click **OK**.

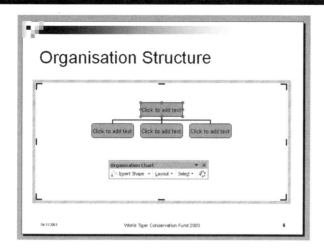

The Chief Executive Officer is Mike Stevenson and he has four Divisional Managers, Mary Wong, Omar Iqbal, Martha Kane and John Hainsworth.

◉ Click in the top box to add some text. Type **Mike Stevenson (CEO)**.

◉ Use the same technique for the other three boxes, adding the names of the first three managers as shown in the figure below:

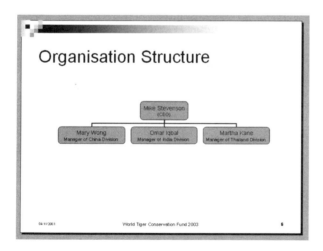

Inserting managers, co-workers and subordinates

We need to add the fourth manager as a co-worker to the other managers.

◉ Click on **Martha Kane** to select the box. The **Organisation Chart** toolbar will be displayed.

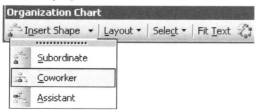

Tip:
Click the down-arrow on the **Layout** button to change the hierarchical layout.

Tip:

There is no option to insert a manager but all managers, except the CEO, will be either co-workers, subordinates or both.

◐ We need the box to be a **Co-worker** type, so click this option. A fourth box should appear. (Alternatively this manager could have been added as a subordinate to Mike Stevenson.)

◐ Enter the name **John Hainsworth, Manager of Siberia Division**.

John has two subordinates, fieldworkers George Bradley and Jo Kemple.

◐ Click on John's box and select the **Subordinate** shape from the Organization Chart toolbar.

◐ Enter the new person's details in the box, **George Bradley, Fieldworker**. Repeat for **Jo Kemple**.

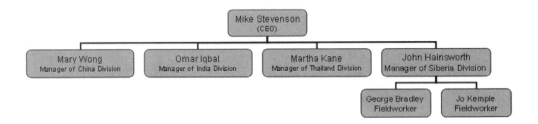

Deleting managers, co–workers and subordinates

The Thailand Division closes down, so we need to delete that manager.

◐ Click on **Martha Kane** and press the **Delete** key.

◐ Jo Kemple, one of John's subordinates and co-worker to George, is fired. Click her box and press **Delete**.

John Hainsworth retires and George is promoted to his position.

◐ Click on **John Hainsworth** and press the **Delete** key. George will automatically be promoted.

Tip:

You can delete any box except the top manager by clicking to select it and pressing the **Delete** key.

Exercise

In this exercise you will apply a design template to the Mapsters presentation you have been working on in the previous practice exercises. You will add footer information to slides and insert an organisation chart.

1. Open the file **Mapsters.ppt**.

2. Apply the **Watermark.pot** design template to the whole presentation.

3. Change the colour scheme to shades of yellow.

4. In the footer of all slides (except the title slide) insert the date and page numbers.

5. Change the position of the page numbers so that they are centred.

6. On slide 4 create the following organisation chart.

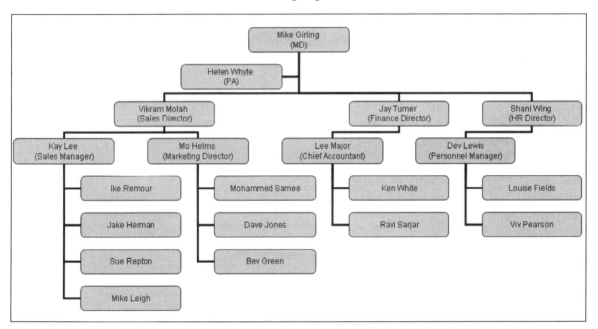

7. Save and close the presentation. You will continue working on this presentation at the end of Chapter 6.4.

Adding Objects

You can add pictures, scanned photographs or cartoons to your documents. You can even put in graphs and charts.

❍ If it is not already on your screen, open the presentation **Tigers.ppt**.

❍ Click on **Slide 5** (shown below) in the **Outline** pane to display it.

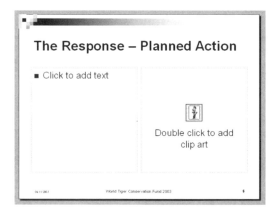

❍ Click where indicated to add text and type **Action at:**. Press **Enter**.

 ❍ Press the **Tab** key or click the **Demote** button. Add the sub-points as shown below:

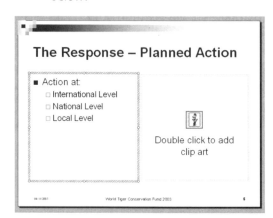

Highlight the text and click the **Increase Paragraph Spacing** button so that the text fills the whole box nicely.

 Click the **Increase Font Size** button to make the text slightly larger.

Inserting a Clip Art image

You may have a CD with some Clip Art you can use. Clip Art is simply a collection of pictures and drawings that have been drawn by professional artists and collected together for other people to use. **PowerPoint** comes with a small collection of Clip Art.

▶ Double-click where shown (on the **Clip Art** placeholder) to add a Clip Art image.

▶ Search for a tiger picture by typing **tiger** into the search box and clicking the **Search** button.

Tip:
Don't worry if you have a different selection of Clip Art – it doesn't matter which image you use.

▶ Click to select a picture then click **OK**. The picture will now appear on the slide.

Tip:
If you change your mind and wish to delete the picture after you have inserted it, simply click to select it and press the **Delete** key.

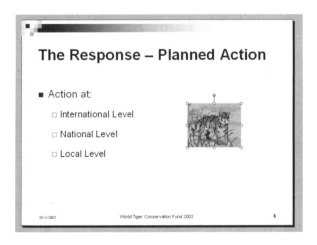

Handles

Note the little circles surrounding the graphic (picture). These are called **handles**. When the handles are visible, the graphic is **selected**.

Tip:
The **Picture** toolbar may appear when the graphic is selected.

- ▶ Click away from the graphic and the handles will disappear.
- ▶ Click anywhere inside the graphic and the handles will be visible again.

Changing the size of a graphic

You can make the graphic bigger or smaller without changing its proportions by dragging any of the corner handles.

- ▶ Make sure the graphic is selected so that the handles are visible.
- ▶ Move the pointer over the top left handle until it is shaped like a diagonal two-headed arrow.

- ▶ Click and hold down the left mouse button. The pointer changes to a cross-hair.
- ▶ Drag outwards. A dotted rectangle shows how big the graphic will be when you release the mouse button. When the picture is about twice as wide, release the button.

Tip:
You can also use this technique to size an image inserted from another file.

Your slide should now look like this:

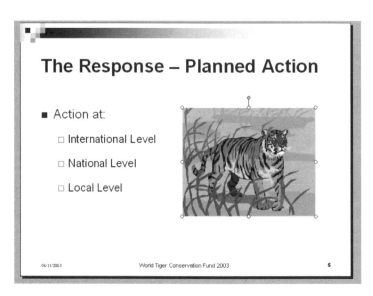

 ▶ Save your work so far.

Copying or moving an image within a presentation

Suppose you wanted this same image on the **Title** slide. We can copy this image across without having to insert another Clip Art image.

- ◉ Make sure **Slide 5: The Response – Planned Action** is selected.

- ◉ Click to select the image. Select **Edit, Copy** from the menu.

- ❶ You could have selected **Cut** instead of **Copy**. This would have copied the image but then deleted it. The **Cut** option is useful when you want to move images, text and slides from one place to another.

- ◉ Go to **Slide 1**. Select **Edit, Paste** from the menu. The image should appear on the slide in a random position.

- ◉ Move the image below the text by clicking and dragging it. Resize it so that it fits nicely.

Tip:
You can copy/cut and paste images that have been inserted from another file in just the same way.
Text can also be copied/cut and pasted within presentations in the same way.

Copying or moving an image between presentations

You can also copy or move text or images (Clip Art or images from other files) between open presentations in a similar way.

Suppose we want to use the same tiger picture in another presentation.

- ◉ Click **File, New** from the menu. Select **Blank Presentation** from the **New Presentation** pane.

○ Go back to the Tigers presentation either by selecting **Window, Tigers.ppt** from the menu, or by clicking the **Tigers.ppt** button at the very bottom of your screen (in the Task bar).

Use these buttons on the Task bar to switch between open presentations

○ Click to select the image. Select **Edit, Copy** from the menu.

❶ Remember you could have selected **Cut** instead of **Copy**. This would have copied the image but then deleted it from the original presentation.

○ Now go back to the new presentation by clicking on it in the Task bar.

○ Select **Edit, Paste** from the menu. The image should appear on the slide. Move and size it appropriately.

○ Save the new presentation as **More Tiger Information** and close it..

Inserting an image to the master slide

We will insert a tiger graphic into the Master Slide for the non-title slides. This can be done by opening the file containing the graphic then simply copying and pasting the image into the slide. You can also import it directly which is what we'll do here.

○ Either find a tiger picture you like from the Internet, or download a couple of tiger pictures from the **Payne-Gallway** web site (**www.payne-gallway.co.uk/ecdl**).

○ Make sure the correct **Master Slide** is in view.

○ Select **Insert, Picture, From File** from the menu.

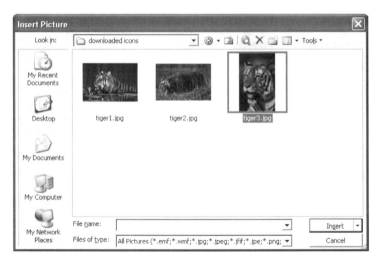

○ Locate the tiger pictures that you've downloaded. Click to select one then click the **Insert** button.

○ Now resize the graphic to be quite small, and position it in a corner.

○ Add a border to the graphic by selecting it then clicking the **Line Color** button. Choose a dark colour.

❸ If you want to delete this image, just make sure you're in the **Master Slide** view, select the image by clicking it, then press the **Delete** key.

You could instead insert a Clip Art picture into the master slide:

○ Make sure the Master Slide is displayed.

○ Select **Insert, Picture, Clip Art**.

○ Search for a tiger picture by typing **tiger** into the Search box and clicking the **Search** button.

○ Click to select a picture and then click **OK**.

To insert a drawn object (such as a shape or a line) into the master slide use the buttons on the **Drawing** toolbar. This is covered in more detail on Pages 6-55 to 6-61.

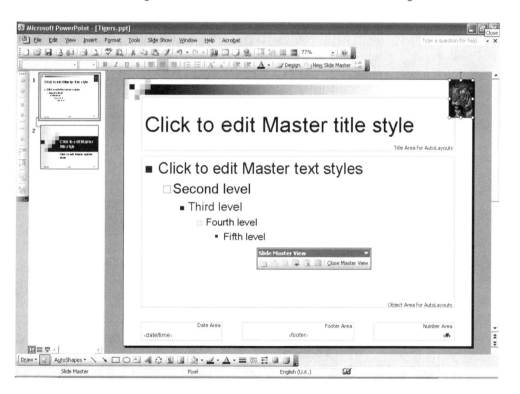

The image will now appear in the corner of all your slides – run the slide show to see!

○ Select **View, Normal** to exit the slide master.

Adding a column chart

We will now add a chart to **Slide 4**. It will show the current population estimates of different species of tigers.

◐ First select **Slide 4** by clicking it in the **Outline** pane. It should already have a **Chart** placeholder as we chose the **Title and Chart** layout in the last chapter.

◐ Double-click the chart placeholder on the slide.

You will then see a small spreadsheet just like you would see in **Microsoft Excel**. Notice that some of the icons on the Standard toolbar have changed.

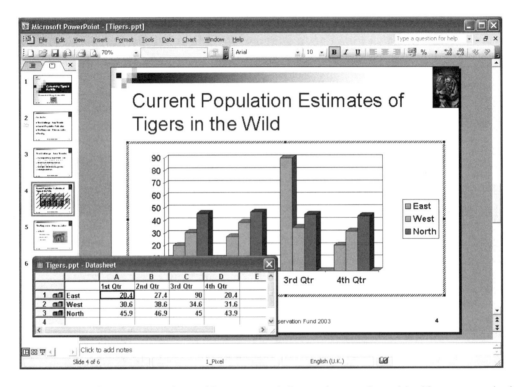

To make the chart you need to add your own information to the table. If you are asked to make a chart in the exam, you will probably be given some information in a table like the one below, and then this information will have to be put into the mini spreadsheet. We'll work through this now.

	Siberian	Amoy	Sumatran
Min. Estimate	360	20	400
Max. Estimate	406	30	500

◐ Click in the cell labelled **East**.

◐ Now begin typing **Min. Estimate**. This will replace **East** with **Min. Estimate**.

◐ Click in the next row and type **Max. Estimate**.

◐ Now do the same for the column headings. Click in the cell labelled **1st Qtr** and type **Siberian**.

◐ Type the remaining two column headings from the table above.

We don't need the last column or the last row, so they need to be deleted.

◐ Click the column header **D** to select the whole column.

◐ Press the **Delete** key to delete all the values from these cells.

◐ Now click in row header **3** to select the whole row and press **Delete**.

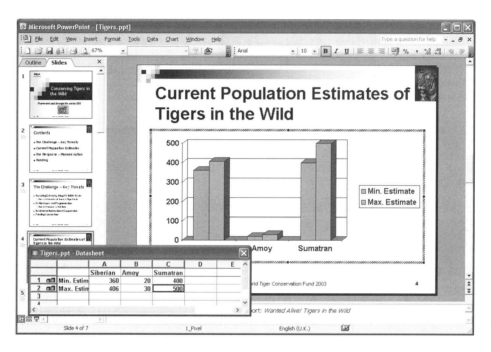

Now we need to enter the correct figures.

◐ Replace the figures already in the spreadsheet with the ones in the screenshot below, or from the table above.

		A	B	C	D	E
		Siberian	Amoy	Sumatran		
1	Min. Estim	360	20	400		
2	Max. Estin	406	30	500		
3						
4						

◐ Close the table by clicking the **Close** icon. Click somewhere on the slide outside the chart area to deselect it.

Your chart should now look like this:

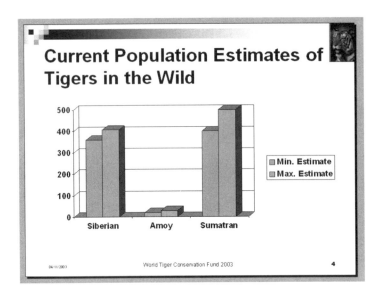

Sizing a chart

To adjust the chart size, click it and drag a corner handle inwards to make it smaller and outwards to make it larger.

Editing a chart

Suppose you have made a mistake in one of the figures or headings in the chart.

○ Double-click the chart. The datasheet appears again. If the datasheet doesn't appear, just right-click on the **Chart Area** and select **Datasheet** from the menu that appears.

Tip:
The **Chart Area** is the dark blue area around the chart. To be sure you're in the right place, just hover the mouse pointer over that area and the **Tool Tip** will tell you where you are.

○ Click away from the datasheet and it will disappear.

Changing the colours of the column chart

You can change both the background colour and the colour of the columns.

Changing the background

○ Double-click the chart so that the datasheet appears.

○ Right-click in the middle of the chart (where the **Tool Tip** says **Walls**), then select **Format Walls** from the menu that appears.

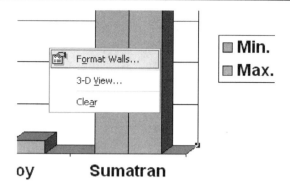

oy **Sumatran**

The **Format Walls** window appears.

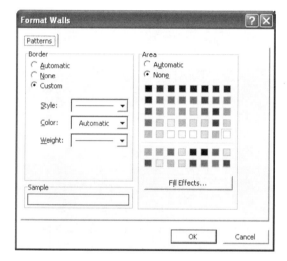

O Click one of the colours to select a background colour, or check the **None** box to leave the background transparent. Click **OK**.

Changing the column colours

O With the chart still in edit mode (with the datasheet visible), right-click on one of the columns, then select **Format Data Series** from the menu that appears.

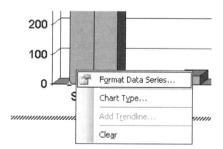

The **Format Data Series** window appears.

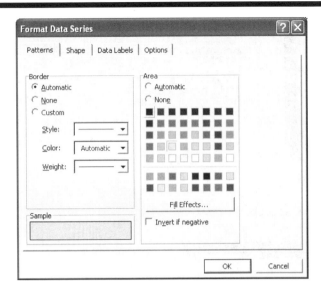

● Pick a different colour for the data series then click **OK**.

❶ This will only have changed the colour of one of the data series. To change the other colour, right-click on the column that you want to change.

Adding a pie chart

We will create a new slide that will have a pie chart. The pie chart will also be based on the tiger population estimates.

● In the **Outline** pane, click to select **Slide 4** then select **Edit, Copy** from the menu.

❶ You could have selected **Cut** instead of **Copy**. This would have copied the slide but then deleted it. The **Cut** option is useful when you want to move images, text and slides from one place to another. To delete a slide, click it to select it and then press the **Delete** key.

Tip:
You will learn how to copy or move slides between open presentations in Chapter 6.6.

● Now select **Edit, Paste** from the menu. A copy of **Slide 4** should appear just after **Slide 4**, and has become **Slide 5**.

● Double-click the chart on **Slide 5** to show the datasheet. We only want the minimum estimates to be included in the pie chart, so delete the row named **Max. Estimate**.

Tip:
You can cut or copy just the chart to move or copy it to another slide or another open presentation. Click the chart and select either **Edit, Cut** or **Copy**. Move to the destination slide and select **Edit, Paste**.
To delete a chart, click it and press the **Delete** key.

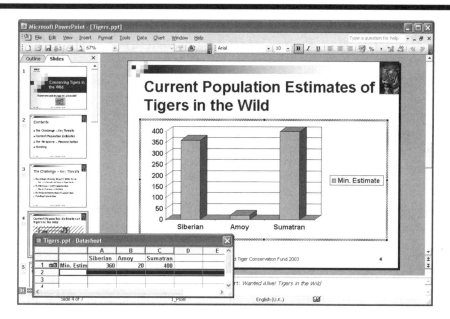

● Now we need to change the chart type. Right-click on the Chart Area (outside the actual chart, but within the chart boundary).

Tip:
If **Chart Type** isn't on your menu, you probably clicked in the wrong place.
PowerPoint brings up different menus according to where you click.

● Select **Chart Type** from the menu that appears.

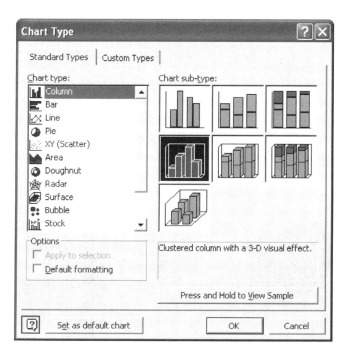

○ Click **Pie** in the left-hand window of the Chart Type dialogue box. You are given a choice of different pie charts, but the one already selected is fine so click **OK**.

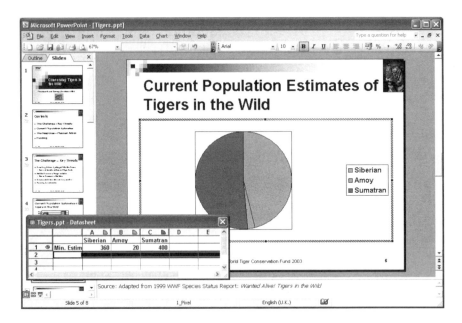

The chart is now a pie chart!

❶ If you want to add some data labels to the pie chart, like a percentage next to each slice, right-click somewhere under the legend whilst the datasheet is in view, then select **Chart Options** and change the settings under the **Data Labels** tab. You'll need to do this whilst the chart is selected; if you can see the datasheet then the chart is selected.

○ Have a play with the suggestions mentioned above. Your chart should now look something like this:

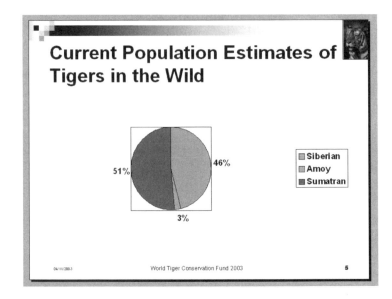

Changing chart colours

We looked earlier at how to change some of the colours in a column chart. All chart types can be formatted in a similar way. First of all take a look at some of the other chart types such as bar charts and line charts:

◉ Double-click the pie chart and select **Chart Type** from the pop-up menu.

◉ Select a type from the list and then click the **Press and Hold to View Sample** button.

To change the background of any chart, make sure the datasheet is in view, then right-click close to the chart within the background (the **Plot Area**). Select **Format Plot Area** from the pop-up menu and choose a colour from the **Format Plot Area** dialogue box.

You can change the colour of all columns, bars, lines or slices within a chart or you can change individual items. The technique is the same for column, bar, line and pie charts. For example in a bar chart:

To change the colour of all the bars in a data series, select the chart, click a bar once, right-click and select **Format Data Series** from the pop-up menu. Select a colour from the **Patterns** tab on the **Format Data Series** dialogue box.

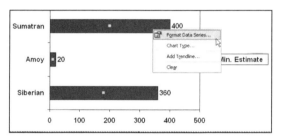
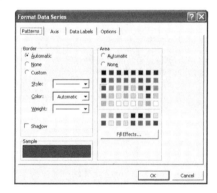

To change the colour of an individual bar, click any bar once, then click the specific bar to select it. Now right-click it and select **Format Data Point**. Select a colour from the **Patterns** tab on the **Format Data Point** dialogue box.

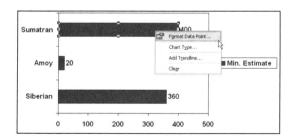
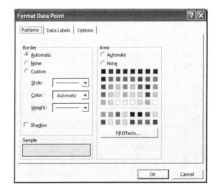

Exercise

Now you will add a graphic to the Mapsters presentation you have worked on in previous practice exercises. You will also add a chart showing the company sales by product (i.e. maps of European countries).

1. Open the file **Mapsters.ppt**.

2. Find a Clip Art image of a globe that would be suitable as a company logo for Mapsters Ltd.

3. Insert it on every slide except the title slide, in the top right-hand corner.

4. Size the image to fit.

5. On the Sales by Product slide insert a pie chart based on the following information:

			A	B	
			2002 (£k)		
1		Austria	60.9		
2		Belgium	89.4		
3		Eire	86.7		
4		France	170.4		
5		Germany	120.4		
6		Italy	130.9		
7		Portugal	86.3		
8		Spain	140.3		
9		Switzerland	98.9		
10		UK	80.6		
11					

Mapsters.ppt - Datasheet

6. Give the chart a title and display the data labels as percentages. Run the slide show. Save and close the presentation.

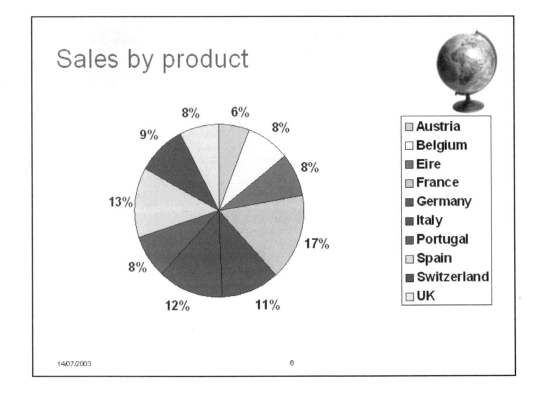

Special Effects

In this chapter you will be adding sounds and animation to your presentation. You can also add transition effects when each screen opens.

◉   Open the presentation **Tigers.ppt**.

◉   Select the **Slide Sorter View** and click the first slide.

Adding Slide Transitions

Transitions change the way a slide opens. You can make the next slide open like a blind or a curtain, for example.

All the commands you need to create transitions are in the **Slide Transition** Task pane.

◉   To view this pane click **Slide Show**, **Slide Transition** on the menu. Alternatively, if the Task pane is already visible, you can bring up the **Slide Transition** options by clicking the small down-arrow at the top of the Task pane, then clicking **Slide Transition** from the menu that appears.

◗ With the first slide selected, scroll down the list and select **Split Vertical Out**. This will make the first screen open like a curtain, as if it were opening in a theatre.

◗ You can also add a sound to this transition by simply choosing one from the **Sound** list.

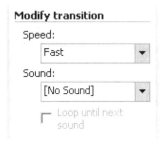

You can also change the speed at which the transition occurs. In most cases, **Fast** is the best. Try experimenting!

Adding transitions to multiple slides

If you wish to add a transition to all the slides, click the **Apply to All** button in the **Slide Transition** pane.

You can apply a transition to more than one slide but not all by selecting the slides first using the **Ctrl** key, or **Shift** to select a range.

To add the same transition to all the rest of the slides except **Slide 7**:

◗ In **Slide Sorter View**, click **Slide 2** and then hold down the **Shift** key.

◗ With the **Shift** key still pressed, click **Slide 6**.

◗ Now choose the **Cover Left** transition from the **Slide Transition** pane.

◗ Now view your show to see the results!

Tip:
When you start a Slide show, it will start from the currently selected slide. If you want to start from the beginning, make sure **Slide 1** is selected before clicking the **Slide Show** button.

Adding special effects to text

PowerPoint also allows you to add animation effects to objects such as Clip Art images, charts and bulleted lists.

In **Slide Sorter View** you can add animation using the **Slide Design** pane.

◗ View the **Slide Design** pane by clicking the small down-arrow at the top of the Task Pane, then selecting **Slide Design – Animation Schemes** from the list.

◗ At the top of the **Slide Design** pane, make sure **Animation Schemes** is selected.

●   Click away from the slides to deselect them, then click **Slide 2**.

●   Click to select an animation effect from the **Slide Design** pane. If you don't like it, just click another one.

●   Try out your chosen effect in **Slide Show** view.

●   Go back to **Slide Sorter View** and change the animation effect to **Dissolve in**.

Formatting text and images

Now we will create the logo of the World Tiger Conservation Fund.

Most of the tools we will need to do this are on the **Drawing** toolbar. This is usually located at the bottom of the screen in **Normal View**.

Tip:
These tools can also be used to draw objects on the master slide.

Adding a shadow to text

●   Select **Slide 1**. Click the **Text Box** button on the Drawing toolbar.

●   Click and drag the mouse button to draw a text box near the top of the slide.

●   Enter the acronym **WTCF** in Arial, bold, size 24.

●   Click the **Shadow Style** button on the **Drawing** toolbar.

●   Click to select one of the shadow options – it doesn't matter which one.

Adding lines to a slide

We'll add a horizontal line beneath the letters.

> Click the **Line** button on the **Drawing** toolbar.

> Whilst holding down the **Shift** key, click and hold the mouse button to drag out a horizontal line. Release the mouse button when you are happy with the line.

> The **Shift** key restricts the number of angles the line can take which makes it easier to draw a horizontal line. Try drawing it without!

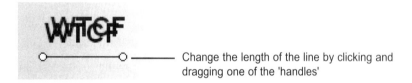

Change the length of the line by clicking and dragging one of the 'handles'

> If you want to move the line slightly higher or lower, move the mouse pointer over the line until it becomes two double-headed arrows, then click and drag.

Changing the colour of the line

> Click the line to select it. Click the small down-arrow on the **Line Color** button.

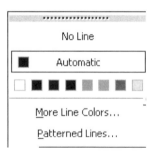

> Click to select a different colour, such as a dark blue.

Modifying the line width

 Click to select the line. Click the **Line Style** button.

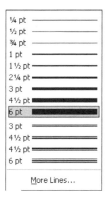

Make the line much thicker by clicking the **6pt** line.

Modifying the line style

 With the line selected, click the **Dash Style** button. Select one you like from the list.

That's all we need for the logo, but let's practise using some of the other drawing tools.

Adding a free-drawn line

 Click the **Autoshapes** button on the **Drawing** toolbar.

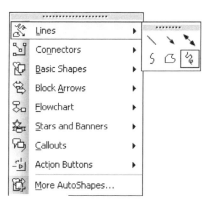

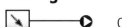 ▸ Select **Lines**, then select the **Scribble** icon.

▸ Add a freehand scribble to the slide!

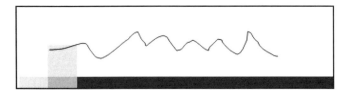

Adding an arrow

 ▸ Click the **Arrow** button on the **Drawing** toolbar.

▸ Click and drag out an arrow next to your freehand line, then release the mouse button.

▸ Format the arrow by right-clicking it, then selecting **Format Autoshape** from the menu that appears.

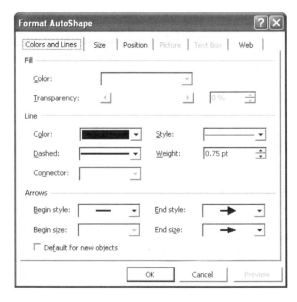

The **Format Autoshape** window appears:

▸ Change the arrow beginning and end style until you are happy with it. Click **OK**.

Rotating or flipping an object

 ──●   Now flip the arrow you've just drawn. Make sure it is selected, then click the down-arrow on the **Draw** button on the **Drawing** toolbar.

● Select **Rotate or Flip** from the next menu.

● Have a play with the different rotate and flip options!

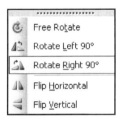

Selecting and grouping drawn objects

● You can select more than one object by clicking the first object, holding down the **Shift** key, then clicking other objects. Select the freehand line and the arrow you've just drawn.

❶ Grouping objects is useful if you want all the separate objects to be treated as one object. This means you only need to click once to select them all, and if you move one of the objects, all the others will be moved too.

● With both the objects selected, right-click on any one of the objects.

● Click **Grouping**, **Group** from the menu that appears.

The objects are now grouped! Try selecting them and moving them around – they should move together.

Ungrouping

- To ungroup, just right-click one of the objects and select **Grouping**, **Ungroup** from the menu that appears.

- Now group the 2 lines together again.

Sending objects to the front or back

When you've got two objects overlapping, **PowerPoint** will automatically place the most recent object on top. If this isn't what you want, you need to change the **Order** of the objects, and either send one of the objects to the back, or bring one to the front.

- Drag the objects you've just drawn so that they are overlapping the text on the title page. You should see that the objects are on top of the text.

We'd like the text to be on top, so we will send the drawn objects to the back.

- Right-click one of the objects and select **Order**, **Send to Back** from the menu.

The objects will now be behind the text!

- Bringing the text to the front would have had the same result. To do this, select the text box so that it has a fuzzy border, then right-click the border and select **Order**, **Bring to Front** from the menu.

 Drag the lines away from the text and press the **Delete** key to remove them from the slide.

Adding shapes to a slide

As well as lines, you can add a range of shapes such as boxes and circles to a slide. You can modify these shapes in exactly the same way as lines. We'll run through this quickly by adding a rectangle at the top of the slide.

- Click the **Rectangle** button on the Drawing toolbar. Click and drag the mouse pointer to drag out a large rectangle like the one below:

Tip:

 Use the **Oval** tool to draw ovals and circles. To draw a perfect circle or square, keep your finger on the **Shift** key as you drag out the shape.

Changing the fill colour

 ➤ Make sure the rectangle is selected and click the small down-arrow on the **Fill Color** button.

➤ Select a dark blue colour.

➊ If you didn't want any fill in the shape, you would choose **No Fill** instead of a colour.

Changing the border colour

 ➤ Click the **Line Color** button and make the border the same dark blue as the fill.

Applying a shadow to a shape

This is done exactly as for the line.

 ➤ Click the **Shadow Style** button then one of the shadow options.

➤ Now tidy up the title slide by deleting the shape you have just added: just click to select it then press the **Delete** key.

Moving or copying a line or shape

To move or copy a drawn object, click the object and select **Edit, Cut** or **Copy**. On the destination slide (either within the presentation or in a different, open presentation) select **Edit, Paste**.

Deleting a line or shape

To delete a drawn object on either a normal slide or the master slide, click the object and press the **Delete** key.

Aligning a line or shape on a slide

To align a drawn object on a slide, click the object and then click the **Draw** button on the **Drawing** toolbar. Click **Align or Distribute** and make sure the **Relative to Slide** option is selected. Now select how you want the shape to be aligned (e.g. left, right, centre etc.)

Tip:
Click the **AutoShapes** button on the Drawing toolbar to access lots more shapes such as stars, banners, triangles etc. These can be drawn, formatted and deleted in the same way as rectangles and circles.

Adding and modifying a text box

We will add a text box to **Slide 5**.

- ◉ With **Slide 5** selected, click the **Text Box** button on the **Drawing** toolbar.
- ◉ Click and drag the mouse button to drag out a text box anywhere below the chart.

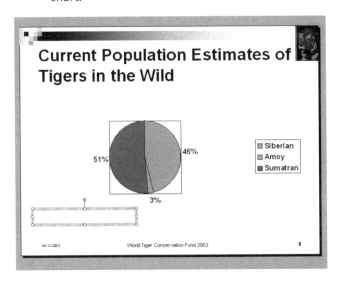

- ◉ Type the text **Source: 1999 WWF Species Status Report**.

Repositioning and resizing

- ◉ Click and drag the handles until the text box is positioned as shown below:

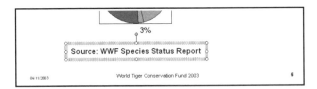

Changing the text colour

- ◉ Select the text box so that it's got a fuzzy border. Click the down-arrow on the **Font Color** button.

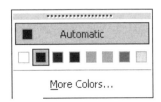

- ◉ Select a dark blue colour.

Adding a border

○ Click the **Line Style** button. Select the **1pt** line.

○ You can change the colour of this line using the **Line Color** button.

Adding superscript and subscript text

We will add a superscript **1** to effectively footnote the **Source** text box.

○ Add the number **1** directly after the title, without a space.

> # Current Population Estimates of Tigers in the Wild1

○ Highlight just the **1**, then select **Format**, **Font** from the menu.

○ Check the box marked **Superscript**.

❶ If you wanted to add **subscript** text, you would check the box marked **Subscript** instead.

○ Click **OK**. The **1** should now be in **Superscript**.

> # Current Population Estimates of Tigers in the Wild[1]

○ Now add a **1** before all the text in the text box. Make it superscript using the same method. It should look like this when you're done:

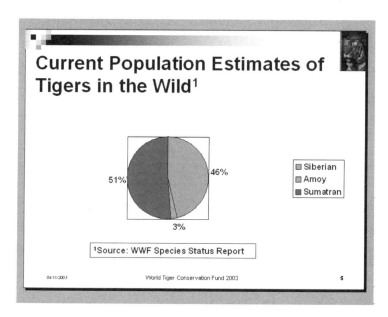

Exercise

There is just one slide left to complete on the Mapsters Ltd presentation that you have been working on at the end of each chapter. This exercise asks you to complete that slide and add slide transitions and special effects.

1. Open the file **Mapsters.ppt**.

2. On slide 5, **Target Markets**, use the Drawing toolbar to produce the following diagram:

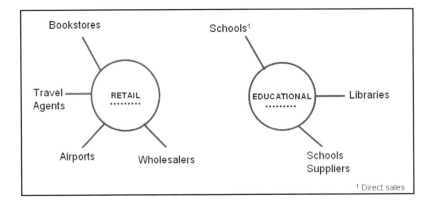

3. Add a **Blinds Horizontal** transition between all slides. Choose to advance slides on a mouse click.

4. On slides 2 and 3 insert a special effect that makes the bullet points fly in from the left at a medium speed.

5. Add a slight shadow to the headings on all pages.

6. Run the slide show and make any necessary adjustments. Save and close your work. The slides should now be looking something like this:

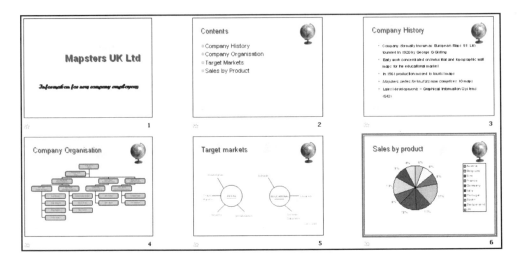

Show Time!

In this chapter you'll find out how **PowerPoint** can help you during your presentation. Most of these features work best when you are giving the presentation on a big screen and controlling it from your computer. That's when **PowerPoint** presentations are most effective.

 Open the document called **Tigers.ppt** if it is not already open.

Starting a show on any slide

To start a show on a particular slide, all you need to do is make sure that slide is selected before clicking the Slide Show button. For example, to start a show on **Slide 3**:

 In the **Outline** pane click to select **Slide 3**.

 Click the **Slide Show** button.

The slide show should open on **Slide 3: The Challenge – Key Threats**.

The Challenge – Key Threats

- **Poaching Driven by Illegal Wildlife Trade**
  - **Ban on International Trade of Tiger Parts**
- **Habitat Loss and Fragmentation**
  - **Human Pressure on Habitats**
- **Inadequate International Cooperation**
- **Funding Constraints**

07/10/2003   World Tiger Conservation Fund 2003   3

Navigating your way around a presentation

○ Once in **Slide Show** mode, **right-click** the mouse and a small menu will appear.

❶ To find your way around a presentation you can click the **Next** and **Previous** options on the pop-up menu. This will take you to either the next or previous step in the presentation.

Tip:
An easier way to go to the next slide is to click the **Space** bar. To go back a slide press the **Backspace** key.

○ If you want to move to a particular slide, click **Go to slide** on the menu. This will bring up another menu in which you select **By Title**. Go to the **Contents** slide.

Hiding slides

Suppose that you don't want to show one of the slides in your presentation. We will hide **Slide 5**.

○ In **Normal View**, select **Slide 5** by clicking it in the **Outline** pane.

○ Select **Slideshow**, **Hide Slide** from the menu.

This slide will now not appear when you run your presentation. You can see in the **Outline** pane if a slide is hidden because it will have the **Hidden Slide** icon behind the slide number.

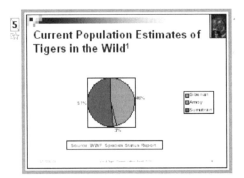

❶ If you want to unhide the slide, follow exactly the same procedure. Just select **Slide Show**, **Hide Slide** from the menu.

Using the Notes pages

To assist you in your presentation you can make additional notes about each slide to prompt you. These notes are visible only by you, not your audience, when you print them out or view them on-screen.

◗ Select **Slide 4: Current Population Estimates of Tigers in the Wild**.

The pane below the slide is for adding notes. To make it easier to write notes, make this pane bigger by clicking and dragging the grey border above the Notes pane.

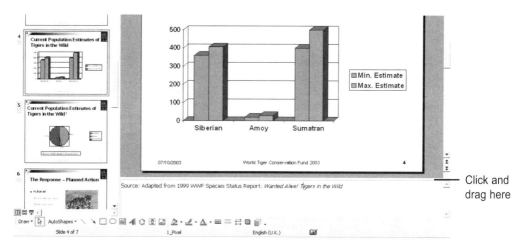

Click and drag here

◗ Now you can type some notes. Type the notes from the screenshot above, or just make up your own.

Viewing your notes during a presentation

You can either view the notes on-screen if you get stuck for words in your show or else you can print out the **Notes pages**. We'll cover printing at the end of the chapter.

ⓘ To view the notes on-screen, right-click the mouse when you're in Slide Show mode and select **Screen** and then **Speaker Notes**. Of course you will only see notes if you are on Slide 4.

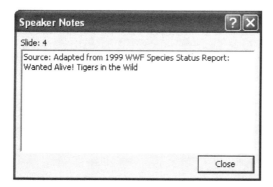

◗ Click **Close** to close the **Speaker Notes** window.

Slide Setup

◗   Select **File**, **Page Setup** from the menu.

❶   To change the orientation of the slides, just select either the **Portrait** or **Landscape** option under the **Slides** section.

❶   You can choose an appropriate output format using the **Slides sized for:** list. The options you may be asked about for ECDL are **On-screen show**, **Overhead** and **35mm Slides**.

If you are printing the slides, change the paper size here

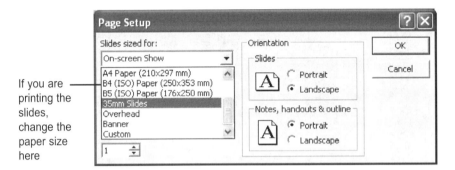

◗   Click **OK** when you are happy with the settings.

Printing

◗   To print anything, select **File**, **Print** from the main menu.

The following window will appear. There are quite a few different options here! Below is a list of things which you may be asked to print for **ECDL**, along with instructions on which options to choose for each.

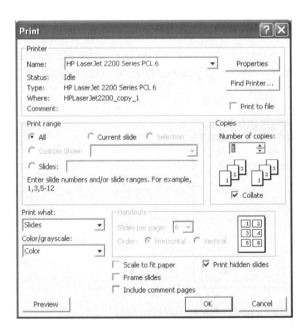

Printing slides

◉ To print just the slides, make sure **Slides** is selected under the **Print what:** section.

◉ You can change which slides are printed using the **Print Range** section.

◉ Set the number of copies in the **Copies** section.

◉ Preview the slide printouts by clicking the **Preview** button. Notice that page numbers appear on the printout because we selected them in an earlier chapter.

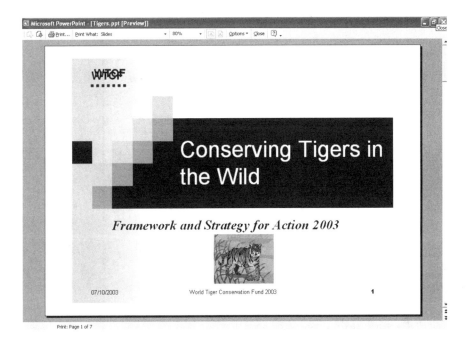

◉ From this screen you can also preview **Handouts**, **Notes pages** and **Outline View**, by selecting the different options under the **Print What:** list at the top of the screen.

◉ Try selecting some of these options to see the different print previews.

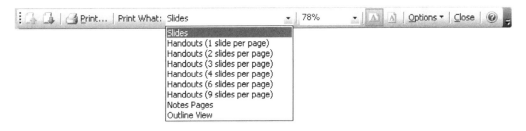

◉ Close the **Preview** window by clicking the **Close** button at the top of the screen.

Printing handouts

◉   This is very similar to printing slides. Select **File**, **Print** to bring up the **Print** window.

◉   This time from the **Print what** list, select **Handouts**.

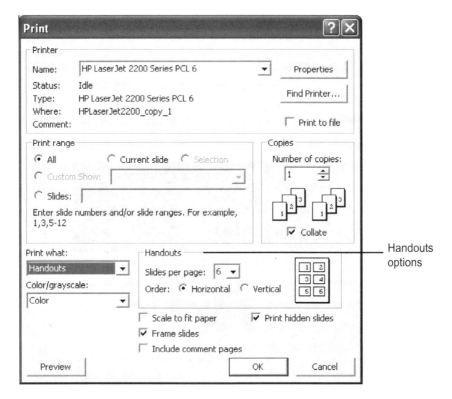

◉   Notice that there is a **Handouts** section in this window. You can choose how many slides to print on a page, and also change the order from **Horizontal** to **Vertical**. Try choosing different amounts of slide per page.

◉   Again, click the **Preview** button to see what it will look like. You can also change the number of slides on a page here using the **Print what** list.

Printing Notes pages

◉   To print the notes, just make sure **Notes pages** is selected in the **Print what** list in either the **Print** window or the **Print Preview** window.

Copying slides to a new presentation

You can copy slides between presentations. To try this out we will open a new presentation – do this whilst keeping the **Tigers.ppt** presentation open.

○   Click **File, New** from the menu. Select **Blank Presentation** from the **New Presentation** pane.

We will add just a couple of slides to this presentation by copying and pasting slides from the **Tigers.ppt** presentation.

○   Go back to the **Tigers** presentation either by selecting **Window, Tigers.ppt** from the menu, or by clicking the **Tigers.ppt** button at the very bottom of your screen.

Click here to select the Tigers.ppt presentation.

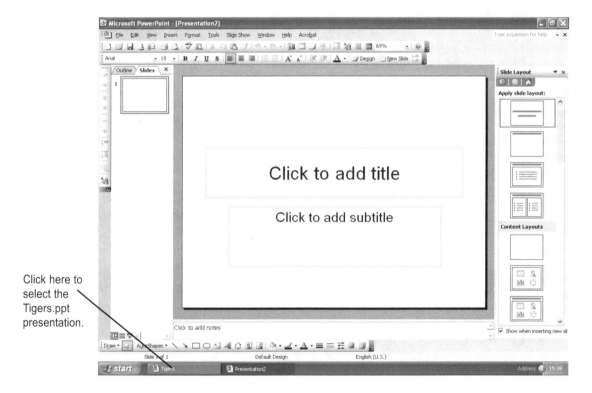

Tip:
Switch between open presentations by clicking the file names on the Task bar.

○   In **Slide Sorter View**, select both **Slide 2** and **Slide 3** by clicking them whilst holding down the **Ctrl** key.

○   Select **Edit, Copy** from the menu.

❶   Remember you could have selected **Cut** instead of **Copy**. This would have copied the slides but then deleted them from the original presentation.

○   Return to the new presentation and click **Slide 1**. Select **Edit, Paste** from the menu.

The two slides will be copied to the new presentation. The background has not been copied because the slides assume the formatting of the new presentation.

 If you want to keep the original formatting, click the **Paste Options** button, which appears under the slides you pasted, and on the button menu, click **Keep Source Formatting**.

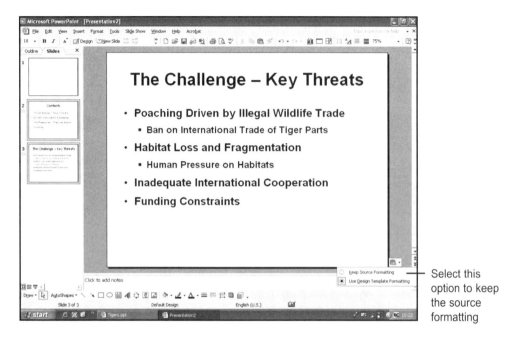

Select this option to keep the source formatting

Tip:
If the **Paste Options** button does not appear, select **Tools**, **Options** from the menu. In the **Options** dialogue box, click the **Edit** tab and select **Show Paste Options buttons**.

○ Save the file as **Tigers2.ppt**.

Saving in different file formats

You have a choice of many file formats other than the normal **.ppt** format. We will save the **Tigers2** file as a template.

○ Go to **File**, **Save As** on the menu. Locate the **Tiger Presentation** folder in the **Save in:** box.

○ Enter **Tigers2** as the **File Name**. Below the **File Name:** box is the **Save as type:** box. There is a large selection of different file types.

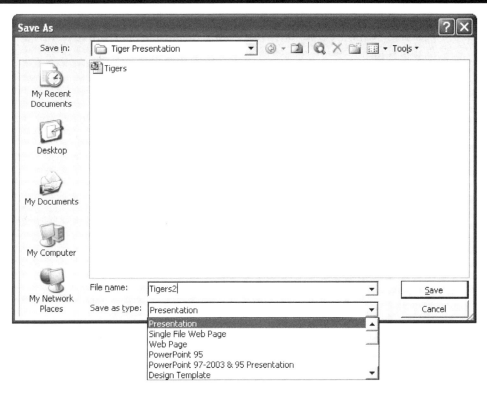

● We'll save this presentation as a **Design Template (*.pot)**. Click to select **Design Template** from the list.

● Click the **Save** button to save the **Tigers2** presentation.

❸ If you wanted to post a presentation to a web site, you would save it with the **Web Page** format (*.htm, *.html).

❸ You can choose to save the presentation for use in a different version of PowerPoint (95, 97-2003 & 95).

❸ If you choose to save in Rich Text Format (*.rtf) you lose the graphical content of the presentation.

❸ You can choose to save a slide as a graphic (*.bmp, *.wmf or *.emf).

❸ You can also choose to save a slide as a graphic for use on a web page (*.jpg, *.png, *.gif or *.tif).

Tip:
To display the **Help** window, just select **Help, Microsoft Office PowerPoint Help** from the menu.

That's it!

You've now finished the presentation – yours should look something like the one below!

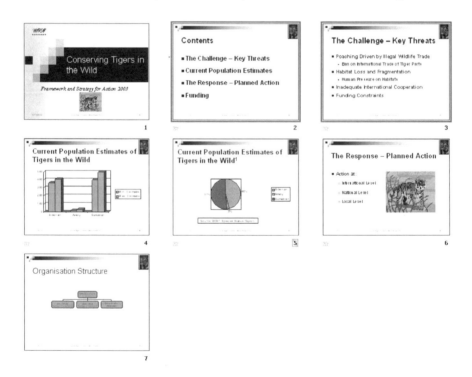

▶ Save and close your presentation, then close PowerPoint.

Exercise

In this exercise you will practise printing the Mapsters Ltd presentation that you have produced in the previous end of chapter practice exercises.

1. Open the file **Mapsters.ppt**.

2. Check the slides in Print Preview and make any necessary adjustments.

3. Return to Normal View and add some notes in the Notes pane of each slide.

4. Run the slide show and display some of the Notes pages.

5. Print the slides on one page of A4 paper in portrait orientation.

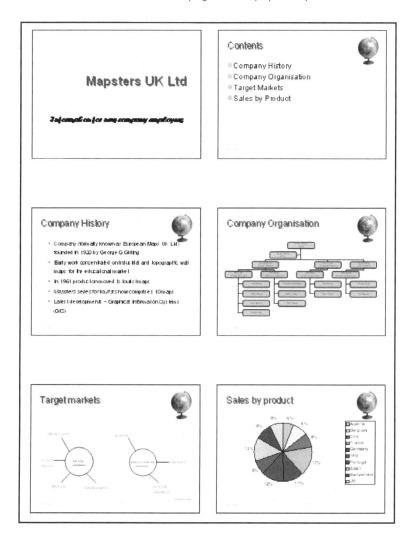

6. Now print the slides on separate pages together with the notes.

7. Save and close your work.